Spotlight on Kids Can Code

What Are
BINARY AND HEXADECIMAL NUMBERS?

Patricia Harris

PowerKiDS press
New York

Published in 2018 by The Rosen Publishing Group, Inc.
29 East 21st Street, New York, NY 10010

Copyright © 2018 by The Rosen Publishing Group, Inc.

All rights reserved. No part of this book may be reproduced in any form without permission in writing from the publisher, except by a reviewer.

First Edition

Editor: Theresa Morlock
Book Design: Michael J. Flynn
Interior Layout: Rachel Rising

Photo Credits: Cover MIXA/Getty Image; pp. 1, 3-4 (background) Lukas Rs/Shutterstock.com; p. 4 Ollyy/Shutterstock.com; p. 7 Maliutina Anna/Shutterstock.com; p. 9 sirikorn thamniyom/Shutterstock.com; p. 11 Everett Collection/Shutterstock.com; p. 12 RomanR/Shutterstock.com; p. 13 showcake/Shutterstock.com; p. 17 HorenkO/Shutterstock.com; p. 19 Melody Smart/Shutterstock.com; p. 21 ProStockStudio/Shutterstock.com.

Library of Congress Cataloging-in-Publication Data

Cataloging-in-Publication Data
Names: Harris, Patricia.
Title: What are binary and hexadecimal numbers? / Patricia Harris.
Description: New York : PowerKids Press, 2018. | Series: Spotlight on kids can code | Includes index.
Identifiers: ISBN 9781508155232 (pbk.) | ISBN 9781508155119 (library bound) | ISBN 9781508154761 (6 pack)
Subjects: LCSH: Computer programming–Juvenile literature. | Binary system (Mathematics)–Juvenile literature.
Classification: LCC QA76.6 H37 2018 | DDC 005.1–dc23

Manufactured in the United States of America

CPSIA Compliance Information: Batch #BS17PK: For Further Information contact Rosen Publishing, New York, New York at 1-800-237-9932

Contents

Number Systems..........................4
The History of Base 10.................6
The Position of Digits.................8
The Binary Number System..............10
Why Use Binary?.......................12
Boolean Logic.........................14
The Hexadecimal System................16
Why Use Hexadecimal?..................18
Coding in Hexadecimal.................20
Using Number Systems..................22
Glossary..............................23
Index.................................24
Websites..............................24

Number Systems

Zero, 1, 2, 3, 4, 5, 6, 7, 8, 9! You probably learned these numbers very early in your life. When American children learn to count, they use a number system called base 10. In this system, the same 10 numbers, 0 through 9, are combined to form higher numbers. The base 10 system isn't used for everything in the United States, but it is very common.

Binary and hexadecimal number systems are used for computer coding. A binary system is a number system in which all numbers are formed using 0s and 1s. A hexadecimal system uses the numbers 0 through 9 and the letters A, B, C, D, E, and F to represent number values.

Binary is also called base 2 because this system uses two symbols to represent all numbers. Hexadecimal is called base 16 because this system uses 16 symbols.

Decimal (base 10)	Binary (base 2)	Hexadecimal (base 16)
0	0000	0
1	0001	1
2	0010	2
3	0011	3
4	0100	4
5	0101	5
6	0110	6
7	0111	7
8	1000	8
9	1001	9
10	1010	A
11	1011	B
12	1100	C
13	1101	D
14	1110	E
15	1111	F

The History of Base 10

Why do we use a number system based on 10? It's probably because humans have 10 fingers! People most likely created the base 10 system because it's easy to use your fingers to count.

The base 10 system was developed using the Hindu-Arabic numeral system created in India during the 600s. The Hindu-Arabic system had symbols for the numbers 0 to 9. The way the numbers look today is based on the Latin **script** developed by the early Romans.

Not all countries use the base 10 system the same way. In the United States, we count past 10 by using new words for numbers, such as "eleven," "twelve," and "thirteen." In China and Japan, instead of using a new word for numbers over 10, "ten" and another number are combined to make a new word. For example, 13 is called "ten three" and 67 is called "six ten seven."

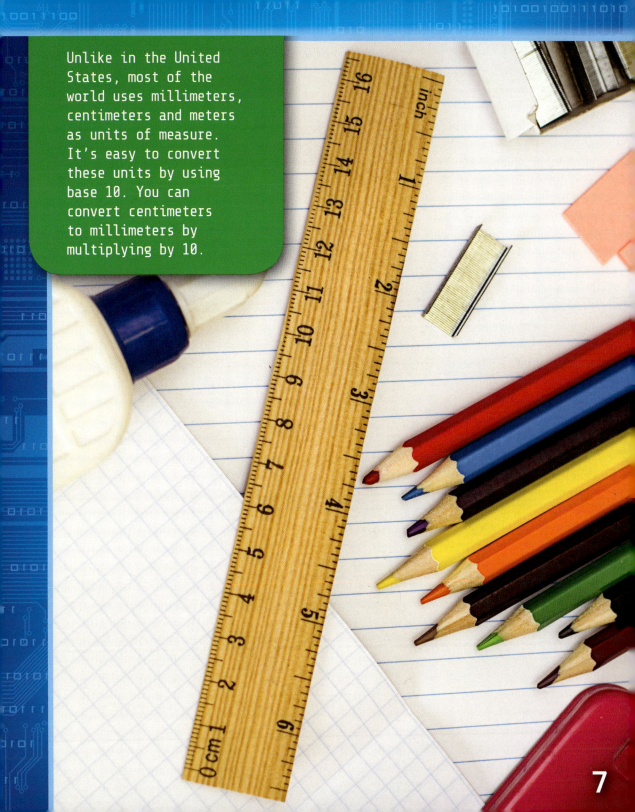

Unlike in the United States, most of the world uses millimeters, centimeters and meters as units of measure. It's easy to convert these units by using base 10. You can convert centimeters to millimeters by multiplying by 10.

7

The Position of Digits

Base 10 uses a **digit's** position to show its value. For example, the number 583 is different from the number 5,803. All digits hold a place in a number. The number 583 is not the same as the number 5,803 because the 0 moves the 8 and 5 into positions of higher value.

You can write very large numbers using the base 10 system because numbers are written based on **powers of 10** such as 100 or 1,000. A digit's position shows you whether it's in the thousands or hundreds.

Base 10 also uses **decimal notation** for small numbers. Decimal notation uses a separator called a decimal point. The numbers to the right of the decimal point are fractions, such as with the number 58.03. In this number the decimal point shows the value of the digits based on their position. The 0 is in the tenths position and the 3 is in the hundredths position.

You must take note of the position of digits to add properly. When adding numbers of two or more digits, you must make sure your number columns line up correctly.

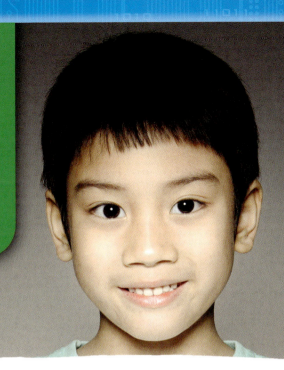

$$\begin{array}{r}1,000\\3,345\\+100\\\hline 4,445\end{array}$$

The Binary Number System

The binary number system, or base 2, is used for computers and computer coding. Just like base 10, the value of a digit in a base 2 number depends on its position in the **sequence** of numbers. When using base 2, there are only two digits to use—0 and 1. So how do we show numbers higher than 1 in this system? It gets a little tricky.

Each number position in a base 10 number is 10 times the number position to the right—ones, tens, hundreds, and so on. Using base 2, each position is two times the number position to the right—ones, twos, fours, eights, and so on.

In base 10, twelve is displayed as "12," a number you are very familiar with. In binary, however, twelve appears as "1100." This can be broken down into 1 in the eights place (or 8) plus 1 in the fours place (or 4), which equals 12.

Postion	Thirty-Twos	Sixteens	Eights	Fours	Twos	Ones
Value	2^5	2^4	2^3	2^2	2^1	2^0
Powers	2 to the power of 5	2 to the power of 4	2 to the power of 3	2 to the power of 2	2 to the power of 1	2 to the power of 0

Morse code is a code that can be used to send messages. The binary number system and Morse code are both systems of communicating with just two symbols. In binary, those symbols are 0 and 1. In Morse code, those symbols are dots and dashes.

Each digit in a binary number represents a power of 2, or 2 multiplied by itself a number of times.

Why Use Binary?

Why is binary used for computers? One reason is that computers use **transistors**. Transistors have just two states: on or off. Although it would be possible to create computers that recognize more than just the on or off state, it would be very expensive to do so. Using the binary system is easy for **hardware** with two states.

The **electric circuits** used for computers don't have on and off states. They have low power states and high power states. These states may vary when the **power input** varies. This varying power is called noise. In computers, electrical circuits are used as binary devices, which means that although the noise changes, the output is not enough to change the on or off state.

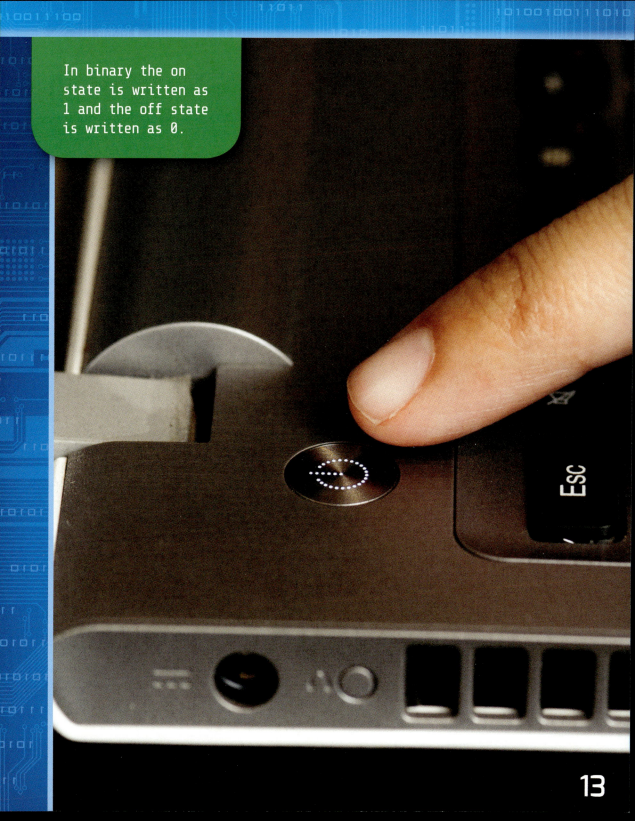

In binary the on state is written as 1 and the off state is written as 0.

Boolean Logic

Another reason for using binary for computers is Boolean logic. Boolean logic is a type of math used in computer coding. In Boolean logic, all values are either true or false. True or false values are combined using the terms "and," "or," "not," and other terms.

Boolean logic gates are used when creating computer systems. The gates NOT, AND, OR, XOR, NAND, and NOR either stop a signal or send it through. In this way Boolean gates have just two operations: stop or send. This fits perfectly with the binary system because all values, true or false, can be represented by 0 or 1. In this way, a Boolean logic gate uses the binary system.

Boolean gates are combined in different ways to complete operations. The math behind these operations is called Boolean algebra. To design hardware, you need a good understanding of Boolean algebra.

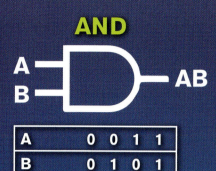

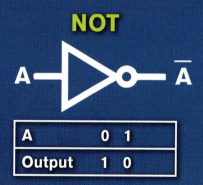

For the three gates, A and B on the left side are the signals that are input to the gate. They can be either send or stop signals: either power on or power off. The right side shows the output of the gate or what it sends on. The table tells whether that output will be a send or stop signal. If the output is 0, it is a stop. If the output is 1, it is a send.

The Hexadecimal System

Another number system used with computers is the hexadecimal system. The hexadecimal system is a base 16 system. That means there are 16 symbols in the system. Hexadecimal uses the common numerals 0 to 9 and the letters A, B, C, D, E, and F (or sometimes lowercase letters) for the six symbols beyond the common numerals.

Like the base 10 system and the binary system, the hexadecimal system relies on the position of the numerals and the letters to show a value. The hexadecimal system uses 1s, 16s (16 to the power of 1), 256s (16 to the power of 2), 4096s (16 to the power of 3), and on up.

Computer programmers began using the hexadecimal system because it was difficult for them to read long binary numbers when checking programs. Programmers use hexadecimal numbers because each hexadecimal digit can represent four binary digits.

You can use your fingers to count from 00 to FF in the hexadecimal system.

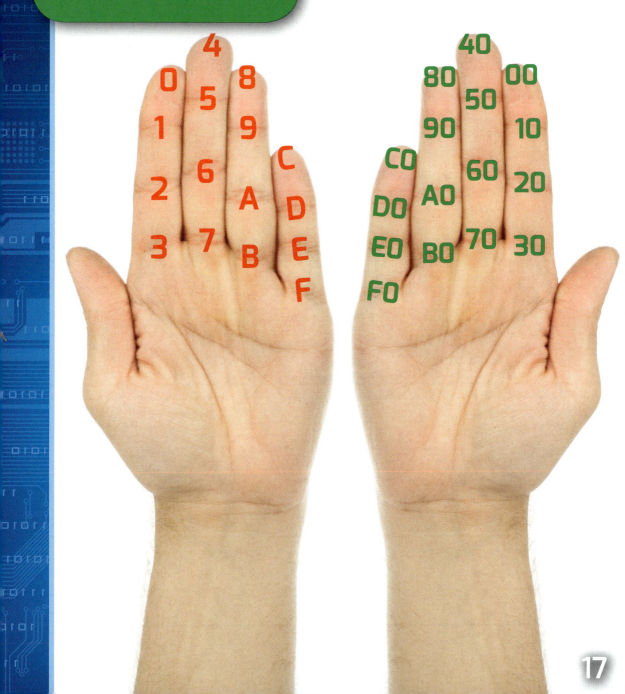

Why Use Hexadecimal?

Hexadecimal is used in **HTML** to represent colors. The color red is shown as #ff0000 in the **RGB** (red, green, and blue) color system. The "ff" stands for the amount of red. The "00" after it stands for the amount of green. The last "00" stands for the amount of blue in the color. Another shade of red is #e52d2d. This shade has less red with some blue and green added.

Hexadecimal is also used to include spaces in **URLs**. If programmers want to include a space in the name of a page, they use the ASCII (American Standard Code for Information Interchange) code for a blank space and write that code in hexadecimal. So, the webpage description at the top of the browser might be: http://www.webpage.com/colors%20for%20webpages. In this URL, the % symbol is used to show that the number is hexadecimal.

Hexadecimal language is still much harder to read than English. Today, programmers are beginning to use hexadecimal less and less.

Coding in Hexadecimal

Hexadecimal can have numbers such as 1,000 that look like base 10 numbers. Certain symbols are used to show that numerals and letters are hexadecimal. In operating systems such as Unix and C, the symbol "0x" is used before a number to show that the number is hexadecimal. So, the number 1,000 in hexadecimal would be written as 0x1000. Sometimes a # or & symbol is used in front of the number. In that case we would see the number 1,000 as #1000 or &1000. Sometimes the **subscript** of 16 follows the number. So, we would see 1,000 as 1000_{16}

Today, many web programmers avoid the use of spaces in their page names by using the underscore symbol (_). The underscore character is an ASCII symbol that can be represented on the screen, and the web address would not use the %20, which would mean using a hexadecimal code. Using the underscore means what appears on the screen is better understood by users than hexadecimal code might be.

Computer programmers use hexadecimal to describe locations and colors.

Using Number Systems

We use the base 10 number system every day. In base 10, one thousand would be written as 1,000. In binary, the system used by computers, 1,000 would be written as 0000001111101000. In hexadecimal, a system used by computer programmers, 1,000 would be written as 3E8. To understand how to read a number accurately, it's important to know what number system is being used. Certain systems are better for certain tasks than others because they may save space or transmit data more efficiently.

You can find binary and hexadecimal calculators online that help you convert numbers between systems. The hexadecimal calculator is often called the hex calculator. "Hex" is an abbreviation that's sometimes used for base 16. You can also find what the number would look like as a word or combination of letters. There are more ways to represent values than you ever imagined!

Glossary

decimal notation: The way numbers are written using nine digits and zero.

digit: One of the elements that combine to form numbers in a system.

electric circuit: A path through which electrical energy flows from one source to another.

hardware: The physical parts of a computer system, such as wires, hard drives, keyboards, and monitors.

HTML: A language that is used to create documents on the World Wide Web.

power input: The electrical energy that is being supplied to a device.

power of 10: Ten multiplied by itself a certain number of times.

script: Written characters.

sequence: The order in which things are arranged.

subscript: A symbol such as a letter or numeral written below or to the lower right of another symbol.

transistor: A small device used to control the flow of electricity in computers and other electronic devices.

URL: The address of a website on the Internet.

Index

A
ASCII, 18, 20

B
base 2 (binary number system), 4, 5, 10, 11, 12, 13, 14, 15, 16, 22
base 10 (decimal number system), 4, 5, 6, 7, 8, 10, 16, 20, 22
base 16 (hexadecimal number system), 4, 5, 16, 17, 18, 19, 20, 21, 22
Boolean algebra, 14
Boolean gates, 14, 15
Boolean logic, 14

C
C, 20
China, 6
colors, 18, 21

D
decimal point, 8
digits, 8, 9, 10

E
electric circuits, 12

H
hardware, 12
Hindu-Arabic number system, 6
HTML, 18

I
India, 6

J
Japan, 6

L
Latin, 6

M
Morse code, 11

N
noise, 12

R
RGB, 18
Romans, 6

T
transistors, 12

U
United States, 4, 6, 7
Unix, 20
URL, 18

Websites

Due to the changing nature of Internet links, PowerKids Press has developed an online list of websites related to the subject of this book. This site is updated regularly. Please use this link to access the list: www.powerkidslinks.com/skcc/bhdc.